FAMILY TRIP TO MAGICAL MADAGASCAR AND BEYOND

FAMILY TRIP TO MAGICAL MADAGASCAR AND BEYOND

BY NICKI GEIGERT

ReadersMagnet, LLC

Family Trip to Magical Madagascar and Beyond
Copyright © 2019 by Nicki Geigert. All rights reserved.

Published in the United States of America
ISBN Paperback: 978-1-950947-75-1
ISBN Hardback: 978-1-950947-76-8
ISBN eBook: 978-1-950947-77-5

All rights reserved. No part of this publication may be reproduced, stored in a retrieval system or transmitted in any way by any means, electronic, mechanical, photocopy, recording or otherwise without the prior permission of the author except as provided by USA copyright law.

The opinions expressed by the author are not necessarily those of ReadersMagnet, LLC.

ReadersMagnet, LLC
10620 Treena Street, Suite 230 | San Diego, California, 92131 USA
1.619.354.2643 | www.readersmagnet.com

Book design copyright © 2019 by Nicki Geigert. All rights reserved.
Cover design by Nicki Geigert
Interior design by Nicki Geigert

High on a hill overlooking the city of Antananarivo, Heather, Sara, Cory, John and Nicki all gather for a photo that marks the beginning of their trip to Madagascar. Madagascar hosts lemurs, fossas, aye-ayes, and a number of other species found nowhere else in the world. A magical land in the Indian Ocean, Madagascar's wildlife is unique, and its forests are full of surprises.

Author: Nicki Geigert

Photographer: Nicki Geigert

ITINERARY

Day 1 (July 1st, 2014): Arrival in Madagascar. Tour for John and Nicki Geigert and family
Hotel: Hotel Lokanga.

Day 2 (July 2nd, 2014): City tour of Antananarivo (B)
Discover Antananarivo, its colorful life, its history and architecture. We spend the morning in the Old City.

Day 3 (July 3rd, 2014): Drive from the capital to the rain forest of Andasibe (B)
We start our journey towards the Eastern part of the island. Enroute we will stop in Marozevo at the Peyrieras reserve.
Hotel: Vakona Forest Lodge.

Day 4 (July 4th, 2014): Explore the rain forest of Andasibe–Mantadia. Hotel: Vakona Lodge Day 5 (July 5th, 2014): Analamazaotra Special Reserve Visit.

Day 6 (July 6th, 2014): Drive from Andasibe to Antananarivo. (B)
We leave the rainforest and come back to the highlands. We return to the capital of Madagascar. Hotel: Relais des Plateaux.

Day 7 (July 7th, 2014): Flight to Morondava. Kirindy's Dry Decideous Forest–Sunset at Alley of Baobabs–Morondava (B, D)
We take a flight to Morondava (MD702 06H20–07H20) Once we land, we will be driven to the Kirindy Forest, home of the Fossa. After our visit, we will head back to the world-famous Baobab Alley to photograph the dramatic sunset over these endemic trees. We drive back to our hotel in Morondava for dinner time.
Hotel: Palissandre Cote Quest Resort & Spa.

Day 8 (July 8th, 2014): Morondava–Miandrivazo–Antsirabe (B)
We will get to the Alley of Baobabs for the sunrise for another opportunity to take some dramatic pictures of this natural landmark. We leave the region of the Menabe to return in the highlands.
In the afternoon, we will reach the town of Antsirabe, known for its thermal waters and rickshaws.
Hotel: Couleur Cafe'.

Day 9 (July 9th 2014): Antsirabe–Ambositra–Ranomafana (B, D)
We continue our journey heading south across the highlands to reach Ambositra, the Malagasy handicrafts capital located 105 km from Antsirabe. In this city known for its woodcarving Zafimaniry Art, we will visit different handcrafter workshops. We will have lunch in this city during which some folkloric dancers and musicians will perform a show. We will drive to the rainforest of Ranomafana.
Hotel: Domaine Nature.

Day 10 (July 10th, 2014): Ranomafana national park: Wildlife photography in the rainforest.

Day 11 (July 11th, 2014): Visit of the tea plantations of Sahambavy & Visit of the Old City of Fianarantsoa Hotel Tsara Guest House Day 12 (July 12th, 2014): Fianarantsoa–Ambalavao–Ranohira (Isalo)

Day 13 (July 13th, 2014): Isalo–Visit of the Isalo National Park Isalo Rock Lodge Day 14 (July 14th, 2014): Ranohira–Toliara–Boat transfer to Anakao.

Day 15 (July 15th, 2014): Close up bird photography in Nosy Ve Hotel *Anakao Ocean Lodge & Spa.*

Day 16 (July 16th, 2014): Transfer to Toliara, Flying back to Antananarivo. *Hotel: Lokanga.*

Day 17 (July 17th, 2014): Fly to Nosy Be Hotel: Ravintsara Wellness Spa.

Day 18 (July 18th, 2014): Lokobe reserve & Sacred tree visit Day 19 (July 19th, 2014): Nosy Tanikely.

Day 20 (July 20th, 2014): Nosy be-Antananarivo (B).
We transfer you to the airport to fly back to Antananarivo
Hotel: Lokanga.

Day 21 (July 21st, 2014): Markets of Antananarivo & International departure.

MADAGASCAR

Madagascar is the fourth largest island in the world. It lies on the eastern side of Africa and is separated from the African continent by the Mozambique Channel, a distance of over 300 miles.

Madagascar is home to some of the most unique and unusual species of wildlife in the entire world and has almost 25,000 species of wild animals with a good number being endangered species.

It was to this place, on June 29, 2014, that the Geigert Family, John Nicki, Heather and Cory, along with grand-daughter Sara Sanchez embarked for the trip of their lives. Sara had just graduated from high school and was set to go to college in the fall of 2014. In the meanwhile, this was her special high school graduation gift from her Oma and Opa.

Sara, Logan, and Mom Laurie had all driven down to San Diego to personally see Sara off on her first international trip. We arrived at the airport, said our good-by and then headed over to terminal 2. After check-in, we sat in the lounge for 3 hours and boarded our plane for an 8:30 PM departure. After dinner and a movie, we were all pretty much ready for sleep as we put our chairs into the horizontal position. Yes, we did fly business class. We arrived in London at approximately 2:30 PM London time, and 6:30 AM San Diego time.

Our next stop was Johannesburg, South Africa, where we had to go collect our luggage and then put it onto the next flight for Antananarivo, the capitol of Madagascar. After 36+ hours, we finally arrived in Madagascar. It was July 1, 2014. We were met by our Guide and Driver, Hery Andrianartenaina. I think that the Malagasy people have the longest names in the world. After we had our luggage, we had to actually fight off the baggage guys, who desperately wanted to be paid for getting our luggage from the terminal to our vehicle. They fought to wrest the baggage carts out of our hands and take over. With 40% unemployment in Antana, these poor guys were just trying to make a living. We then drove for over an hour through rush hour traffic, to a boutique hotel called Lokanga.

When we arrived at the Lokanga Boutique Hotel, people came out to assist with our luggage because we had to walk down a steep stairway, and across the lawn to the entrance. Our room was on the second floor. It had a small desk, chair, TV, vestibule, and a bathroom on the opposite side of the entry.

We had a huge veranda that overlooked the city. Cory's room was perpendicular to ours, so he shared the veranda. Heather and Sara's room was on the third floor, up some very steep stairs to the attic. It was long and narrow, with no windows.

Lokanga sets high on a hill overlooking Antana, which is actually the center of the city. The view is amazing over the city, and the sunset was rich with reds, oranges, and yellows. We all took in the sights, sounds and smells surrounding us.

Between the hotel and the airport, there are fields of rice, carts being pulled by young men and boys, women with baskets of laundry on their heads, young kids along the way begging, brick ovens baking bricks with people hauling them up to the roadside to sell, and a different looking cattle that we have never seen called zebu.

Our meal was wonderful for our first night. There was duck with broccoli and chocolate mousse for dessert. Madagascar is known for their chocolate.

The following morning, we were awakened by the sounds of roosters crowing, dogs barking and children walking by, on their way to school.

And then we also heard bumping and banging noises coming from out on our veranda. I went to see what was causing the noise. It was Cory. He had gotten locked out of his room when the floor bolt had slipped back into the hole when he went out onto the veranda and had closed his door. It was rather funny.

We all had our breakfast and then Hery came to take us to the King's palace. We were told that the first people to arrive in Madagascar 2,000 years ago were probably from India and Malaysia. Others later came from Europe and Africa. They set up a kingdom. They had both a King's Palace and a Queen's Palace, both high on the hills overlooking the city of Antananarivo. On the opposite side of the hill from our hotel, sets King Andrianampoinimerina's Palace. He ruled the Kingdom of Imerina from 1787 until his death in 1810. He had reunified his country after 77 years of war when the country had been divided into 4 parts.

We had to drive past many older French styled homes, and women doing laundry community style. All shared in the washing and the rinsing. In one sense, it is a communal gathering for the women to get together as they work.

The view from our veranda at the Lokanga Boutique Hotel. It overlooks the Royal city of Antananarivo, with a population of 1.4 million people. Madagascar's climate is warm with a rainy season from November to April, and a cooler, dry season from May to October.

So many areas make up the city as a whole. There are even rice fields included within the city boundaries.

There are entire families that make bricks down along the banks of the river or along the rice fields. They need an oven to bake the bricks after they have been formed. Each person has a special job to do.

The bricks are formed from clay mud and straw. Most homes are made from the bricks.

Antananarivo is the capital city of Madagascar set in the central highlands of the country. The city is set between a series of hills, with the royal hill of Ambohimanga overlooking the city from 15 miles away. Ambohimanga is a traditional fortified royal settlement (Rava) that is a northeastern hill.

Both the king and queen palace overlook the city. The royalty are buried in their palatial gardens.

There are 12 hills surrounding the lower town area. The mid-levels are where the nobility used to live. Most houses were constructed of wood but were torn down and rebuilt of stone later in the 19th century. There are soccer fields, churches, and plazas on the lower level. Soccer is very important in Madagascar. Antana has a very large soccer stadium as seen above.

A typical old styled French home in Antananarivo. In 1894 the French invaded, colonized it, and set up a single government. It become independent in 1960.

Steps up to the King's Palace. called the Rava. It is set on Ambohimanga Hill. It served as the home of the kings and queens of the Kingdom of Imerina in the 17th and 18th centuries.

A series of gates and pathways in the Imperial Gardens. The sacrificial stone was for oxen and sometimes children to be sacrificed. It is taboo to point at anything, and can get you into trouble.

This Fig tree was in the Royal Grardens. Because of it's shape, Sara, Heather, and Cory all had to climb it.

UNIQUE ANIMALS OF MADAGASCAR

Most of the species found in Madagascar cannot be found anywhere else in the world. Some of these unique animals are:

A songbird called the Fody, unusual species of Tenrecs, Tomato Frogs, Satanic Leaf-Tailed Gecko, Panther Chameleon, Comet Moth, Fossa, and Lemurs. Over the past 2,000 years, the biologically rich forests of Madagascar have been reduced by almost 90% mainly through agriculture and other commercial activities such as logging. This massive deforestation has pushed several of the island animals to the brink of extinction.

There are over 60 species of lemurs, including the elusive Aye-Aye, and the tiny mouse lemurs, seen only at night! There are more exceptional chameleons and frogs, birds and insects, and plant life than anyone has ever seen. Currently all lemurs are endangered species, due mainly to habitat destruction (deforestation) and hunting. Many are very endangered and have been placed on the Red List of Threatened Species. The bamboo lemur is critically endangered because their habitat forest has been reduced to about 4% of the original size. Madagascar is home to nearly 60 "taxa" of lemurs (species, sub-species, and populations from 33 species across five families and 14 genera) ranging in size from the 25-gram pygmy mouse lemur to the indri.

All lemurs belong to the suborder Strepsirrhini within the order Primates. The 101 extant species and subspecies are divided among 5 families and 15 genera. They range in weight from 30 g (1.1 oz) (Madame Berthe's mouse lemur) to as much as 9.5 kg (21 lb.) (indri).

These are some of the Lemurs that we saw:

- Ring-Tailed Lemur—The body of it is very different from other primates. It is considered to be one of the most intelligent of them as well.

- Red Ruffed Lemur—The Red Ruffed Lemur is a medium sized species. They don't associate with any other types of Lemurs. They seem to turn their noses up at them and won't even nest or feed in the same locations.

- Indri Lemur—The Indri Lemur is also called the Babakoto in many regions. This is one of the largest Lemurs found in the world. They seem to have many behaviors that are humanistic. They have characteristics that are different from many other species of Lemurs.

- Gray Mouse Lemur—It may be hard to believe that the Gray Mouse Lemur is a primate! In fact, many people think that it is a rodent by the name and the appearance of it. Yet DNA doesn't lie and so it is correctly classified as a primate.

- Golden-Crowned Sifika—One of the medium sized primates is the Golden-Crowned Sifika Lemur. They are very limited in number and location. There isn't much known about them and they were only identified as a unique species in 1974.

- Coquerel's Sifika—The Coquerel's Sifika Lemur is medium sized and belongs to the primate family. It features some very interesting behaviors as well as a look that is different from other Lemurs.

- Collared Brown Lemur—The Collared Brown Lemur is a primate that is medium in size. There are 12 species of Brown Lemurs in the world. They are the most well-known of these Brown Lemurs.

- Black Lemur—The Black Lemur is a type of primate and there are two subspecies that have been identified. They are the Slader Lemur and the E. Macaco Lemur. In many locations their ranges overlap and that has led to mixed breeding.

- Aye-Aye—Of all the Lemurs in the world, the Aye-Aye Lemur is the largest primate that is nocturnal. One may argue that point though if they didn't realize that this was really a primate.

- Verreaux's Sifaka—The Verreaux's Sifaka Lemur is medium in size when compared to other species. It is a primate and looks very similar to many small species of monkeys. As a result, it is usually accurately categorized as a primate.

After leaving Antananarivo, we went to the Peyrieras Exotic Preserve off on the N2 in Marozevo, Madagascar. It is approximately 47 miles from Antana. After a nice walk up a fairly steep hill, we came to a family of Verreaux's Sifika Lemurs, and Common Brown Lemurs, along with the Coquerel's Sifika Lemurs. Coqueral and Verreaux's Lemurs look almost identical, and are hard for the amateur to tell apart. These all appeared at different times to be fed bananas, and other fruit by the tourists who stop in to see them.

This was our very first encounter with lemurs. I was so very excited that I could hardly contain myself. Our guide brought bananas for us to give to the lemurs and also picked some loquats from one of the trees along the way. He then called all of the lemurs together. We heard them first and then saw them as they leapt from tree to tree coming closer and closer to us through the tangle of jungle vines, trees and plants. They love fruit, so it is such a treat for them. They don't care who gives it to them, and they will fight over it. The guide showed us all how to hold the fruit so that the lemurs could easily take it from us.

Heather and Sara were ready. The lemurs took it right out of their hands. One lemur was so close to me that I could not resist running my hand down its back. It was so very soft and silky. These are the Coquerel's Sifika (Propithecus Coquerali). We then saw all of the Chameleons.

The Comet moth (Argema Mittrei) or Madagascar moon moth is one of the most beautiful moths in the world. Found only in Madagascar, they are among the largest in the world with a wingspan that extends to 20 cm coming only second after the Atlas moth of Asia. The insect has bright yellow color, a long tail, and is nocturnal. The females are broader, and their wings are rounder, their tail is also shorter than the males. To this day these beautiful animals have no protection status, and their population status has not been established. The eggs of the moth are collected for trade in the world markets. There are no known farms for these insects in the country, and their existences rely on the already protected shelters. The striped Gecko, the tomato frog, and all of the different varieties of chameleons were such a delight to the eyes and so fascinating to watch.

We stopped to eat at a restaurant owned by our Malagasy Guide named Maria, and her brother. She has been the sole support for her family for many years. She is a really great person, and a good guide. Maria showed us through the V.O.O.M.M.A. Community Forest Preserve in Andasibe, and through the Mitsinjo Reserve for a night walk. This was also near the Vakona Forest with the Lemur Islands.

Lemurs are primates that look like an animal that's a combination of a dog, a cat and a squirrel. They have incredibly unique and exciting behaviors that include singing like a whale. There are more than sixty species of Lemurs in Madagascar today that vary in size from 25 gms. pygmy lemurs to the largest Indri Lemurs weighing more than 12 kgs.

Lemurs are one of the most threatened animals in the whole planet and according to IUCN Red List of Threatened Species, 22 species of lemurs are critically endangered, 48 are endangered, while 20 are vulnerable. Sara enjoying her first Black and White Ruffed Lemur.

The trip to Vakona Islands was among our favorite. We had so much fun interacting with the Lemurs. They were hysterical, climbing and jumping all over us, especially when they thought that we had bananas for them. We each got our own photos with the Lemurs. Sara made sure that she had her own, with selfie shots.

By the time that we got to the Ring-tailed Lemurs, it had started pouring rain. Although we had rain gear on, we were still totally drenched in the canoes, with the Lemurs jumping in and out. Lemurs do not like to get wet, so some decided to go into the bush to try to stay a bit drier.

Each one of us so enjoyed the encounters with the lemurs, as well as the other wildlife, such as the snake that only Cory wanted to hold. The rest of us took a pass on that one.

The Brown lemurs are the most aggressive and have no manners when it comes to sharing anything. They love to view their world from atop something, or someone. John can certainly vouch for that.

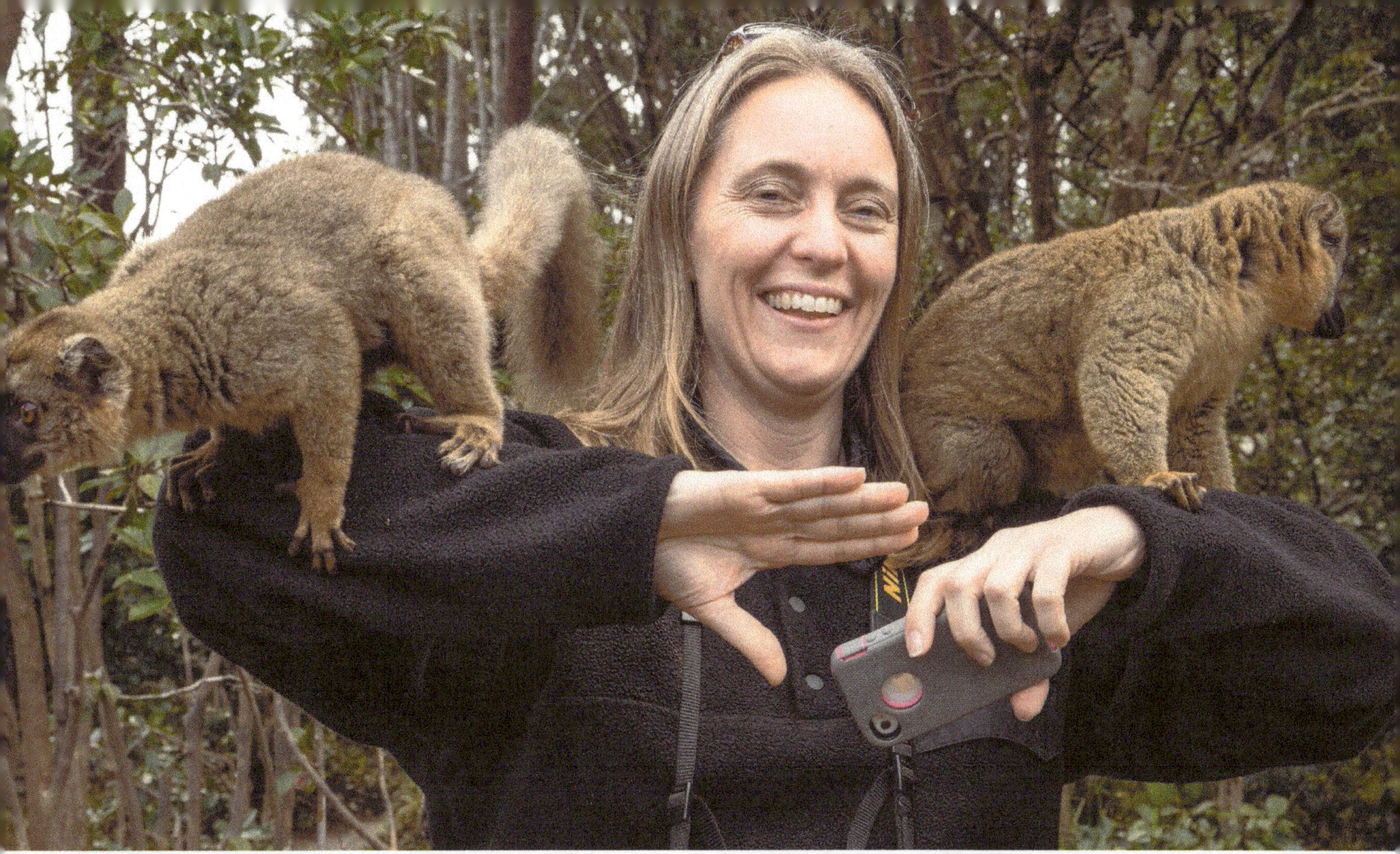

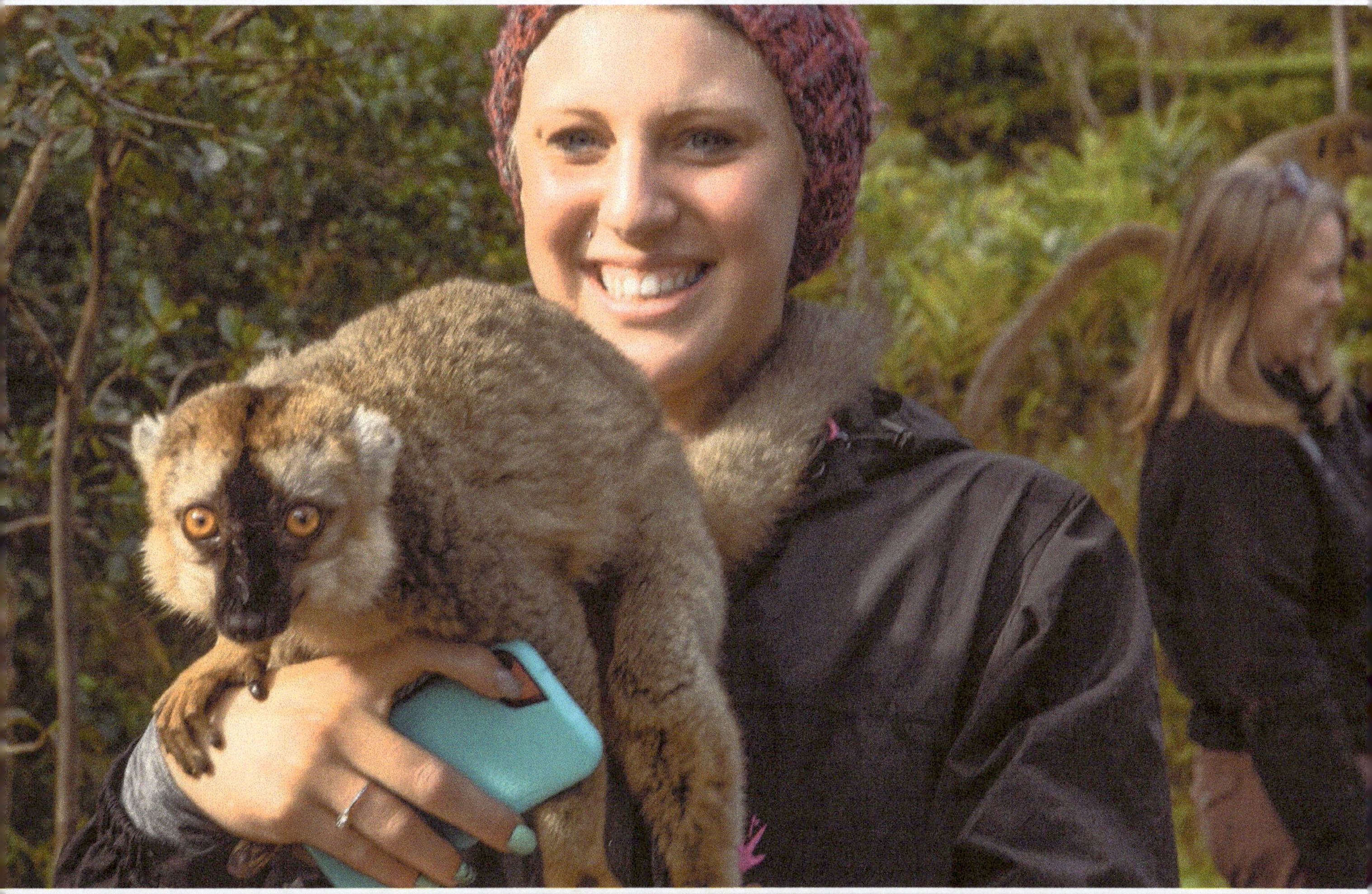

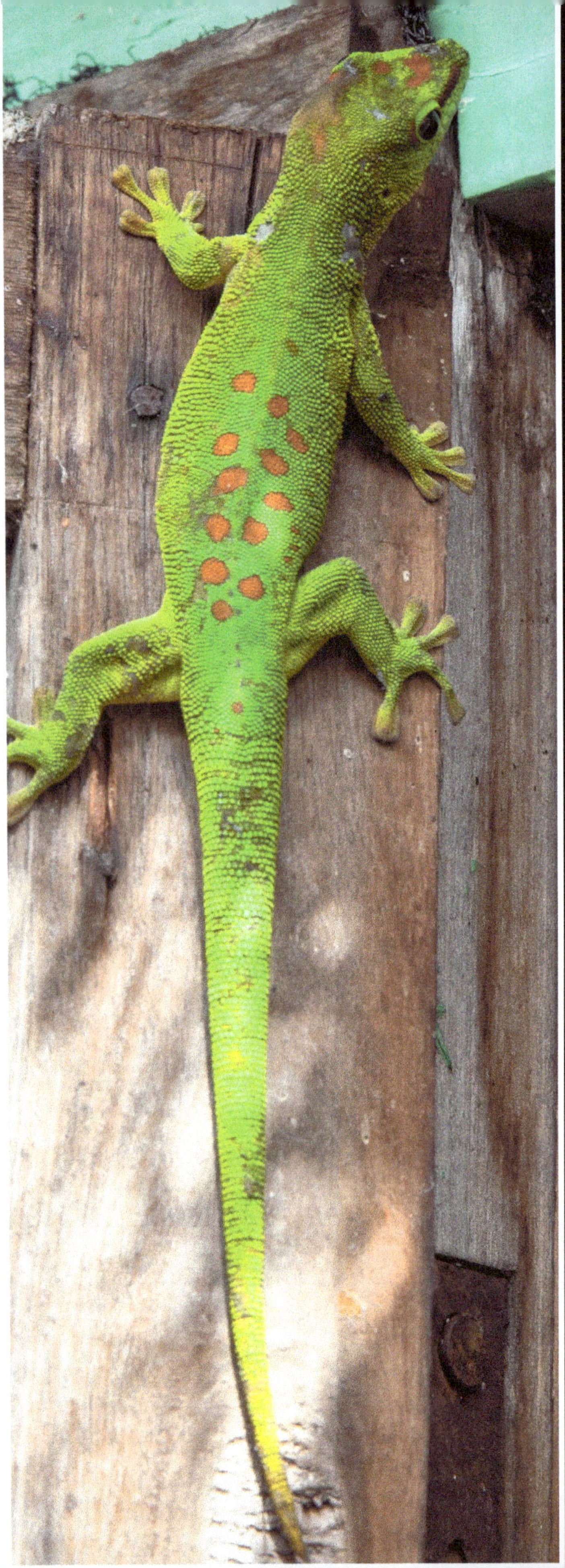

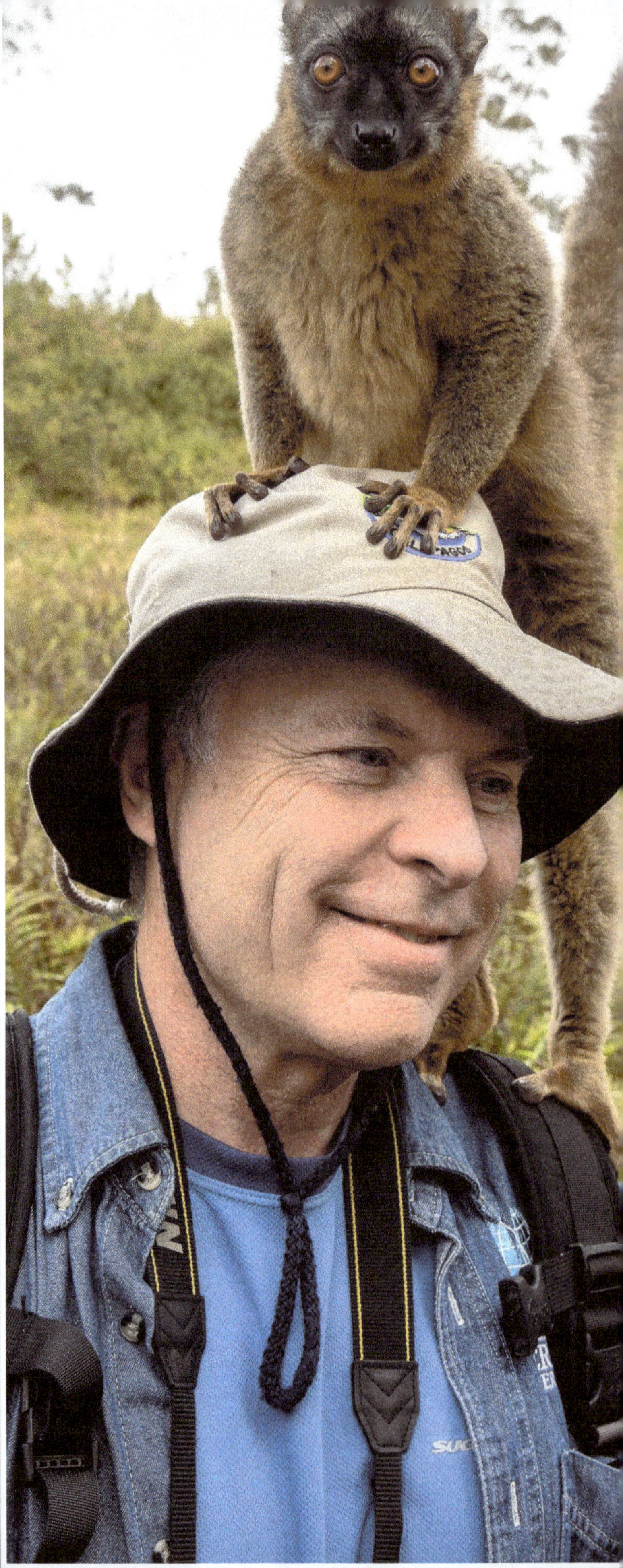

July 6, 2014 After our amazing encounter with the Lemurs at Vakona, we got all dried off, relaxed and played a game of scrabble for the evening. Everyone had to repack all of their bags. The following day we were up at 7:00AM and off to Antana to the airport. Hery came to load everything up, and we were in the vehicle by 9:00AM. After we left Vakona, we went to the village to see the people. Because of the rain, it was hard to take any photos, but the people still came out to do their daily chores and work.

Hery bought some bananas for us to taste. They were so much tastier than Chiquita bananas. Probably because they were tree ripened. We drove through a couple of towns on the way back to Antananarivo. One was called Mora Manga, and the other was Mangora. Mora Manga had a population of about 100,000 people.

That night, of July 6, 2014, we stayed at a hotel near the airport. We were to have a 4:00AM departure, but the flight was delayed until 8:00AM so we were happy about that.

That night we all ate in at the hotel, but the food was nothing to brag about. Hery took our bigger bags so that he could have the driver drive them to Morondava, while we took the plane. It was a good plan and allowed us to simply get on the plane without having to deal with checked luggage. This was our last night together for all 5 of us. After the morning, Sara and I were heading off on our own, and everyone else was heading home.

Sara and I had no choice but to take the Malagasy Airline. It is always notoriously late, and basically undependable. It is a wretched airline. That being said, the 10:00 flight was changed 3 times by the time that the plane finally arrived, and we boarded at 11:30. By the time that we arrived in Morondava, at 12:30, our driver on that end was nowhere to be seen. Everyone else's driver was there, but not ours.

Two taxi drivers asked where we were going, so I showed them my paperwork, and told them that we were going to the Palissandre Cote' Quest Hotel. They said that they knew where that was, so after a call was placed to our driver, with no answer, we asked to two guys to please take us to the hotel. They were very nice to do that. They only had a very tiny Smart car, so we squeezed in. In the meanwhile, our driver called, and said that he would meet us at the hotel. We arrived, and had completed our check in, and then our so-called driver came, full of excuses. He said that since the day was mostly over, that there would be no time for us to see the Kirindy Forest, home of the Fossa. The Forest is a dry forest. There are several kinds of tiny Mouse lemurs that live there. I really wanted to see Baobab Alley for a sunset shot, so that is what I chose for us. The driver just wanted to show up at the last minute, but I was so angry at him that I told him that he was to take us early so that we could see what everything looked like in the light. He was trying to get out of it, but I would not budge. Poor Sara had never seen me so angry at someone. Bottom line, when a person is paid to do a job, and does not do it properly, then they must make certain amends. This guy wanted to do nothing. I did get some incredible sunset shots over the small pond that sat along the eastern side of the Alley.

The following morning, we were up at 7:00AM and ready to go by 8:00AM. Hery had arrived, and I told him how horrible, Patrick, our driver had been. Hery took us to where the "Lover's Tree" was. It was a two-hour drive away from Baobab Alley. It is 2 Baobab trees that had grown together. Sara actually tried to climb them but was unsuccessful. We stopped at a few places to photogragh rice fields and zebu, and other things after leaving Morondava. It was a very short stay, and we had a 10-hour drive ahead of us. We were on our way to Antsirabe.

The road system in Madagascar is horrible. In sections, it is actually not bad, but most of the roads are washed out, or have some major potholes in them. It seemed to take forever as we bumped along. The landscape changed from dry red clay to more green and lush areas, with higher altitude changes. We saw entire families breaking up the rock to pan for gold. They were also shoveling sand out of the river in order to pan it. We saw children watching after the zebu. In some areas there were lots of kids not in school. In other areas we saw lots of kids in uniforms going to school. Everyone was coming or going somewhere. So many people walking along the roadway. It must have been laundry day, for there were clothes hanging on bushes, from lines in houses, everywhere. There was also a soccer game going on in one town.

Our new hotel for the night was the Coulteur Cafe'. The room was great for Sara and me, and the food was good. We were up and, on the road, again by 8:00AM, since we had lots of ground to cover. Sara was a trouper. We headed toward Ambositra, the handicraft capital of Madagascar, located 105 km. from Antsirabe. We stopped to see all of the artisans working on their particular arts and crafts. Sara bought a bowl and a spoon. I bought a bowl. One artisan demonstrated how to make inlayed wood patterns. After 5.5 hours of driving, we stopped for lunch and we were serenaded by a couple of guitar players. Apparently, Haja had requested their services for us, even though we came an hour and a half later than they expected.

The Lover's Baobab Tree Near The Dry Kirindy National Forest.

Wednesday, July 9, 2014—It is in the southeastern part of Madagascar in HAUTE Matsiatra. It contains more than 160.6 square miles. and has several kinds of lemurs that we have not yet seen.

They are: The Red Fronted Brown Lemur, the Red Bellied Ruffed Lemur, and the Black and White Sifika Lemur. There are also some Bamboo Lemurs, however, they are not easily seen because they are so very shy.

When we arrived that evening, after a very long, all day drive, the staff at the resort was waiting for us. Hery had called ahead to say that we would be having dinner there that night.

Thursday July 10, 2014—The following morning, we were out the door at 9:00AM with a new National Park guide named Angelin Gilbert.

Sara and I were driven to the park entrance, and then started the long walk down some quite steep steps. We walked across bridges, up and down paths, everywhere, and in 3 hours' time we had only seen the 3 varieties that I have listed above. Although we saw very few lemurs, we did see a unique long eared Red Squirrel. Hery threw out some fruit and it stopped to nibble it as we watched. We were back up out of the Rain Forest after 3 hours and 45 min. or so of walking.

After that, we went for lunch at a restaurant called the Grenat in one of the villages. We then took a walk through the market, but by that time it was 3:00PM and all of the stalls were starting to close up shop. It was great fun to walk along and take some people shots. Many did not want their images taken, but Angelin told them that he would bring pictures back with him. The problem was that I had to get the images to him. After the market, we took a walk through another town and then headed back to the lodge for dinner and bed and head out of the rain forest the following day. Since it is called a Rain Forest, it was drizzly and wet. Madagascar has 3 main climates: It has the tropical Rain Forest, the Temperate Inland climate, and the Dry desert temperatures in the southern regions.

Friday, July 11. 2014—Although it was John's and my 44th wedding anniversary, he was not around for us to celebrate. Sara and I were ready to go, to head to Fianarantsoa, but Tony, our driver, had manage to get the SUV stuck. He had backed up too far and the right rear tire went down into the ditch. Poor guy had no clue as to how to get it out. After about 30 minutes of wheel spinning, with mud flying everywhere, and going back and forth, I gave a few suggestions to Hery, who told Tony, who was still hopelessly stuck. Hery finally got in the car, and with the help of people pushing, and a rope tied to the right front and other people pulling, Hery finally got the car out of the ditch. Everyone gave a cheer. We handed out some money to all those who had helped, and then we were on our way to the tea plantation in Sahambavy.

By the time we arrived at the Tea Plantation in Sahambavy, it was lunch time… again. I ordered a tilapia fish with veggies, and Sara ordered a cold appetizer of shrimp.

We were to stay the night in Old Town Fianarantsoa. Soon after we arrived, Hery wanted to show us the view of the city, the old Catholic Church, and the Protestant Church. We climbed up a high high hill, overlooking the city. Along the way, kids were trying to hand us flowers and then ask for bon bon, which means candy. They also wanted to sell us flowers, pictures of the city and anything else that they could think of, to sell us so that they could earn a bit of money. I kept putting off all of these kids by saying "no thank-you" or "Maybe later" to get them to move on.

When I told 3 tween aged boys, "Maybe later", they were very astute, and managed to run all the way back to where the cars were and told me that it was now "later". I bought 1 photo from each one of them, the equivalent of 50 cents each, or 1,000 Aviary each.

Saturday, July 12, 2014—This morning we were up at 6:40 to be on our way to Isalo. I was definitely looking forward to more lemurs, as well as sapphires and diamonds and a silk farm in the town of Ambalavao. They were growing thousands of silkworms and feeding them well with Mulberry leaves. That is the ONLY food that they can thrive on and grow their cocoons. We were shown how they wet the white silk cocoon and then unwind it by machine. The dark brown shell cocoon was put into the water and stacked one into the other. After it was softened, it was then boiled for 30 minutes and then put into the fresh new water. Then the mass of cocoon was taken, and threads were pulled out and hand rolled to make a single strong thread. This was then dyed and put onto a loon for weaving into cloth for a scarf or clothing.

We finally had reached the Anja Reserve in Isalo. We had left the highlands and had descended into the dry plains with fan Palm trees, also called Bismarck Palms. There are Dypsis palms that look like they are growing in an arid spot, but there is always a water source where they grow.

We saw some very small Ring-tailed Lemurs. I commented to Hery about their size and he said that it was all about the diet. Later we drove to the town of Ranohira to go to the gem store that Hery had recommended. We saw nothing good to buy so headed by to Isalo Rock Lodge. Both Sara and I loved this place. The food was excellent, and the 2-bedroom suite was beautiful with full glass windows that overlooked the rocks.

The tea plantation was huge, and was near the Lac Hotel, where we had our lunch. Because there were no workers in the field, we went through the factory to see how the tea leaves were dried, graded, and packed into bags. Then, of course we were taken into the sales room and encouraged to purchase something. I bought 2 bags just because I liked the embroidery on the bags. It was of lemurs of course.

After that, we drove for an hour or more to Fianarantsoa to see the old home and churches that the English missionaries had built as well as the churches that the Catholic French missionaries had built. The house to the right is one example. And again, there is laundry hanging everywhere. Too funny.

Each of these groups had a part in translating the Malagasy language into writing, and then teaching the people about the Bible and Jesus and God's love. In Madagascar today, most of the people identify as being Christian, and only 6% identify as being Muslim. There are also many people groups who still do ancestor worship.

Hery said that the missionaries came to be friends at first, and to teach, but then later brought the soldiers in to take over and to rule the people. I told him that was the Catholic way but not the Protestant way.

We had also encountered people along the way who wanted to know our names. When Sara said her name, they would smile and say that they knew that word. In Malagasy it is Tsara with an "ah" sound, as in arm. The word means GOOD or NICE. Then people would always comment on her eyes. They would say "Good eyes".

Some thought that she had ghost eyes. Those were the ones who worshiped ancestors. They would stare at her eyes and whisper among themselves. We would ask Hery what they were saying.

Isalo National Park is in the Ihorombe Region of Madagascar. It is known for its wide variety of terrain, including sandstone formations, deep canyons, palm lined oases, and grasslands. This particular view is from the high rock mountain formation at the Isalo Rock Lodge in the Sandstone Mountains of Rahohira. The view from the lodge of the deep red rock formations at sunset is stunning. It is in south western Madagascar. When we had arrived, the sun was beginning to set so we literally ran up to the top of this rock to catch the last rays of the sun. We thought that it actually looked a bit like a moonscape. We had also met our new Guide, Andrianirina Charles Fortuna (Nirina for short).

July 13, 2014—After our hike to the top of the mountain to take some photos, Sara and Nirina hiked down the mountain and headed south toward the picnic area. Hery and I went to the SUV and were delayed by about 20 minutes because of a funeral procession. This mountain is a very important sacred place for people to bury their dead. There were at least 200-300 people in this particular procession. The woman was a very important person in her village. We had seen a pile of rocks about half way up the mountain and Hery said that each person in a funeral procession was to pick up a rock to make a wish with and carry it to the place of the burial where they would make their wish and then place the rock around the dead person. After 3 years, the village women would come back and remove the body from under the stones, wash the bones and then rebury the body in a permanent place.

When we finally got past the funeral procession, we had to cross over a deep river area and then parked in the parking lot.

From there, we hiked to the picnic area, and were met by Sara and Nirina. There were lots of people there already, each with their own cook.

I was excited to see 3 new kinds of Lemurs. Of course, they were little beggars, and some were outright thieves, stealing the food right off of the tables. We had to watch everything closely.

The first lemur was the white Verreaux Sifaka, (sometimes called the dancing Sifaka) since its hips are a little different than other lemurs and it can't move well on all 4's.

After lunch, Sara continued her walk up through the canyon, and to the water falls with Nirina. Sara took a swim in each. One was very cold, and the other much warmer. She probably ended up walking 6-8 miles. Hery and I went back to the Lodge.

When it was close to sunset, Hery drove us to a place called "Window Rock". We were there by 4:30 and I set up my camera in the prime position. Then everyone else began to arrive. We waited for the sun to set. One Spaniard thought that he was special, or something, He wanted me to move so that he could get a shot of the entire rock wall with the window shot in the middle. He actually told me to move, and not nicely either. His wife thought that she had to translate for me, but I did understand, and eventually, I did move when I had gotten my shots. We also saw the beautiful grasslands and the vibrantly colored rocks in the distance, along the road to the window rock.

Our next stop was to be on the Island of Anakoa. This is a fishing village of about 3,000 people on the Southwest coast of Madagascar, and south of Soalara.

34

July 14, 2014—After leaving Isalo, we drove through many villages and towns, including one that Hery called Rum town. The children were very dirty and were also involved in making the rum in huge oil drums. There were many fires burning with lots of smoke and sooty looking people. It was probably the saddest sight that we had seen to date in all of Madagascar. We finally arrived in a town called Toliara by 9:00AM. It is a relatively new city by the sea and developed by a French Architect. We boarded a boat which took us an hour and a half to a place called Anakao.

We were greeted at the beach by various porters and the reception manager. We were then escorted to the dining area for a clean face cloth to refresh our face, and a refreshing drink, and then escorted to our bungalow. Our bungalow was right on the beach and had an upstairs and a downstairs. Sara claimed the loft upstairs and I was happy below. We stowed all of our bags in the closet and along the wall and then went out for a walk along the beach. It was great fun watching the little sailing boats and pirogues. We got to sail in several pirogues, some with motors, some with sails. A pirogue is a long narrow canoe made from a single tree trunk, and sometimes has ballasts attached to the sides to give it better stability.

Sara and I went for a walk along the beach. It turned into a bit of an ordeal, with kids, hair stylists, and all kinds of other people harassing us to try to sell us something. We were accosted by these 2 hairdressers, who convinced Sara that she should have some kind of a braid in her very short hair style. I guess that you could say that we were supporting the economy, since Sara told them to go ahead. It cost the equivalent of $5 for them to play with her hair. We continued our walk down the beach and then rather than run the gauntlet of all the people bothering us, we went back to our bungalow via the street and got a bit lost. Another time we walked the opposite direction, away from the crowds, and one guy still pursued us to try to sell us something. I ended up being a little rude to him, just to make him go away. We walked to the point where the land ended-completing a crescent, and then went a different direction toward the fishing villages. We stopped short of actually visiting the people of the village. It was more fun to just beach comb. After our walk, I was hungry and Sara wasn't, so I went to the restaurant and ordered a calamari appetizer. It was the best that I had ever tasted.

The tide was still out so we saw sea life galore. I had never seen such a beautiful Red Knobbed starfish such as the one on the opposite page. It was so unique with red pointy spines. There were many starfish that were left stranded when the tide went out. We threw a bunch back into the water so that the birds wouldn't eat them. There were many seashells and other things to see along the beach also, as well as birds picking up whatever was edible. We had also seen fishermen bringing fish that they had caught, up to the restaurant. At least we could know that the fish was fresh. We also saw this beautiful sailboat sailing by.

The tide was in and the little sailboat that we were in was riding high on the water. This is the kind of boat or pirogue that the fishermen use. We did go to a fishing village at one point. The fishermen keep their nets in great shape. They have to if they want to catch any fish. The net is the tool of their trade, and they must mend it and keep it clean and ready to go each day.

July 15, 2014,—We were up early with our snorkel gear in hand and ready to go to Nosey Ve Island, which was a bird sanctuary. Nosey Ve is sacred to the Vezo people, where each year locals sacrifice zebu according to traditional rituals. This is a breeding colony to the world's most southern all-year colony of red tailed tropic birds. Our day visit had been arranged in Anakao, and we hired a fisherman pirogue. There really was to be no one living on the island, but when we arrived, we saw a family that looked like they had just been dropped off there, to wait for a ride to who knows where. My thought was illegals.

When we landed, we walked to the top of the hill from the beach and then our boat guide, Demitri, helped us find the various nesting birds. Our boat driver, Stephani stayed with the boat.

Dimitri was a bit bored and lazy. He would walk along and point to a bird's nest, or a bird. That was it. We walked for about an hour, and not only took photos, but also picked up pretty seashells. After about an hour, we walked back down the beach and got into the boat and took off to do some snorkeling on a reef. We headed as fast as the wind in the sails would take us. When we arrived at the reef, we jumped into the water. We saw a dying reef that had some sea urchins, brain coral, but not many fish.

These guys didn't know as much as they should have about the tides, tacking, and being aware of wind patterns. We got stranded about a half mile from the shore, so we had to get out of the boat and walk through the water back to our villa in Anakoa. We definitely got our exercise. We were starved so we went for a late lunch.

The market is the most important event of a community. It is where the village people go to gather information as to events and what is going on in the world, and to catch up with the happenings of friends and family. Although many people in other parts of Africa have cell phones, most of the Malagasy people do not. Most of the women still carry baskets of rice and other produce on their heads. They have a special round crown that sets on their head and then the basket sets down in that, which makes it easier to be stable and to carry something. Generally, there are 2 market days during the week. Many are on Wednesdays or Thursdays and also Saturdays.

Some markets are more sophisticated than others. The ones here are very nice, clean markets, compared to those by the roadsides. Depending upon the time of year, there is any variety of foods taken to market. If one lives in a fishing village, then fish and shrimp and other sea things are sold.

We stopped to see some coffee beans growing and Sara was ready for some.

The people of Madagascar are divided into 22 main tribes. I found this fascinating from the standpoint that the people were named based upon where they lived. Each tribe also has many different customs and traditions that differ from neighboring tribes.

For example, these are the Tribes:

1. Antifas Tribe = People of the Sands
2. Antaimora = People of the Coast
3. Antaisaka = Subgroup of Sakalava
4. Antankarana = Rock People
5. Antambahoaka = Tiny sub Tribe of Antaimora of Arabic origins
6. Antandroy = People of the Thorns
7. Antanosy = People of Fanjahira Island
8. Bara = Cattle raisers and Cattle thieves
9. Betsileo = Rice growers
10. Betsimisaraka = The Inseparables
11. Bezanozano = Many plaits
12. Mahafaly = Taboo or Happy makers
13. Makoa = Slave descendants
14. Merina = People of the Highlands
15. Mikea = Foragers and of common background of fleeing from slavery
16. Sakalava = People of the Long Valleys
17. Sihanaka = People of the Swamp
18. St. Marians = Indonesian origin with Arab and European pirate influence
19. Tanala = People of the Forest
20. Tsimihety = People who don't cut their hair
21. Vezo = Fishing People
22. Zafiman = Wood workers, sub tribe of the Betsileo Tribe

Nosey Be is an island off of the northwest coast of Madagascar. It is the largest and busiest tourist resort in all of Madagascar. It has a pop. of 73,000 people, and is 123.56 square miles. The people are primarily fishermen, and the women grow vegetables. Because there are no roads across the island, we took a pirogue boat around to the other side of the island to take a walk through the Lokobe National Rainforest.

We landed close to the beach. The tide was in. The forest Guide was in another pirogue, and was quite large, so we had to give him and the cook a tow in. The homes are made of various barks, grasses, woods, and of course thatched roofs. The guide said that he had the island set aside 25 years ago, so that no one would slash and burn and destroy it. This is one of the only places that the black lemur is found.

While on the island, we saw a leaf tail (crocodile) chameleon, a nocturnal brown lemur, the green panther chameleon, and we were thoroughly bitten by mosquitoes. Very annoying buggers. After our trek, we came back to the little fishing village of Ampasipohy where some of the ladies had their wares and table clothes set out. Sara and I each bought one: a blue one for her Mom and a burgundy one for me. The cook that we had brought with us had also prepared a very nice lunch for us. It was time to go. The tide was out, so we had to take off our shoes and walk through the squishy mud back to the pirogue, and then Arthur wanted to take us to the top of Mont Passot, the highest mountain in Nosey Be. This was the most northern route of Madagascar. The new Ranger station, and new buildings were just being built. We had to walk down in order to walk up to the top. On our return, back in the pirogue, we saw 2 fishing pirogues with fishing nets all rolled up and ready to catch fish.

July 16-17, 2014—The Manga Loa Lodge is a beautiful series of villas on the island of Nosey Be, set on the side of a hill, overlooking the Indian Ocean. When we arrived, we were met by our new guide, Arthur Hassani Bezara. We had flown in from Antana, as usual and landed at the Nosey Be airport, which was south of the Lodge. Because we had arrived in the dark, being very late, we asked for some bananas. That would be our meal for the evening. The waves crashing on the rocks below us, during the night, kept us from getting a good night's sleep. We were surprised at the large numbers of mosquitoes that literally ate us alive during the night. Haja had given this accommodation to me to try it out, because it was new to him.

We had one night there, and we switched to a place called Ravintsara. Upon leaving, we thanked our hosts and then our new guide, Arthur showed us a variety of plants and trees along the way to Ravintsara. We also saw the Ylange Ylange tree, which is the tree that produces the mother flower from which all true perfumes are made. We went via Hellsville, which was actually named after a French military officer and engineer.

We were finished with our hiking through rain forests, so I gave my boots to Hery, and asked him to give the boots to someone who needed them. On the return trip to Antana from Isalo, Hery stopped at a cassava field, where he saw an old man digging the ground up with a shovel. Hery walked out with the boots and they fit when the old man put them on. He had never owned boots in his life. He was very happy.

July 19, 2914—This is our last full day in Ravintsara. Arthur and our driver, Jean picked us up at 8:30 AM to take us to the harbor in Hellville. We got on a motorboat to go across the Mozambique Channel to Nosey Tanikely, which is a Marine Reserve just off the island of Nosey Be. The word "Nosey" means island. When we landed, we saw an adorable female Black Lemur in one of the 3 big shade trees on the beach. I took quite a few shots of her. Arthur told us that her family had been killed by the Brown Lemurs, and she was the only one left. We spent the day hiking around the other side to see Fruit Bats, and then snorkeling in the beautiful pristine water. We were enjoying the beautiful water so much, when, all of a sudden, both Sara and I started getting stung by little Jelly Fish. They were tiny but all over the place. We finally gave up trying to find an area with no Jelly Fish and went back to shore.

We got all packed up after lunch and got back into the boat, heading to Hellville Harbor. Arthur wanted to show us the Sacred Tree, which was a Banyan Tree that had been planted by a Hindu lady several hundred years ago. This tree was the only Banyan tree on the island. Sara and I had to put on a strange sari type of thing called a ceremonial covering, and enter barefooted, with the right foot first. It was blistering hot, so that was the last thing that we wanted to put on. There were small cut out areas in the middle of the hanging tree roots where different people had things dedicated for their dead loved ones to take with them in the afterlife. I guess they have never heard that you can't take anything with you.

After flying back to Antananarivo from Nosey Tanikely, I had asked Hery to take us to the zoo so that we could see all of the other varieties of Lemurs that we had not seen on our trip. Not only did we see Lemurs, but the very first animal that we saw, upon entering the zoo was a Fossa. I watched as one of the zookeepers threw a chicken in and the Fossa went after it as if it had been starving to death. He devoured it almost alive. If we had been able to go to the Dry Kirindy Forest in Morondava, we may have had an opportunity to see one in the wild. The zoo was the next best thing.

Fossa inhabits the forests of Madagascar and is a close relative of the mongoose. It grows to a length of 6ft (1.8 m) from the tail to the nose and weighs up to 26 pounds (12 kgs). The animal has a slender body and appears more like a cat with little resemblance to their relative, the mongoose. The Fossa uses it long tail like a tightrope walking pole to move swiftly through trees. Fossa is among the endangered species and listed by IUCN on the Red list of the threatened species because their habitat is diminishing. Today less than 10% of the original forest cover of Madagascar is in existence which is also the only home of the Fossa.

Hery not only took us to the zoo, but he also talked the zookeeper into letting us go behind the scenes to give the Lemurs their mid-morning snacks of honey and fruits. The Lemurs were beside themselves with anticipation. Sara had no idea what to expect when the Lemur keepers had Sara sit down with her back to each of the green doors. The Lemur keepers put a bit of honey on her cheek and in her hand and then opened the cage door. Out they came as quick as a wink. They were all over her and licking everywhere that there was honey.

It was so much fun to photograph Sara with all of the different Lemur varieties. There were male and female Red Bellied Lemurs (above), a male Black Lemur and female Blue-eyed Black Lemur, (which is really a rust brown, middle photo). The Crowned Lemur, with a rusty looking half-crown on its head, (middle left photo), and 3 Common Brown Lemurs, (Top center). I was amazed at how small they actually are.

July 21, 2014—After a wonderful morning at the Antananarivo Zoo, playing with the Lemurs, we had to make a dash for the airport. Getting through the airport was a serious pain… Because they had major restrictions on economy, they didn't like the weight of my suitcase. I had to take several things out. That meant that my extra weight had to go to Sara's weight, which really made no sense. It all would have come out the same. Neither Sara nor I were happy about that, but we carried on. My camera bag by itself was seriously overweight and the agent took my passport, and had me put my bag on the scale, and then he told me that my bag was overweight. I said of course it was, it's camera gear and I had been carrying it all over Madagascar, and the I could not possibly check it, and could I have my passport back please. Hery said something to him, so he then reluctantly gave me back my passport and we proceeded to the gate. Hery is the best. He is a super guide.

When we arrived in Johannesburg, we were easily checked through to Harare and then on our way. After arriving in Harare, we went to baggage claim and waited for our bags. Sara's bag came, and then we waited, and waited, and waited for my bag, and then they shut the belt down. I knew that we then had a problem. I had to go to the lost luggage window, and the guy was getting up, ready to leave. I told him that I needed assistance since my bag had not yet arrived. He had me fill out some paperwork and then I left with Heather. I was very thankful that I had left some of my clothes behind at Heather's from my previous trip. I was so happy to see Heather, and was also hoping that I would be getting my stranded luggage the following day. I did get it back 2 days later.

July 22, 2014—Today was our first day with Heather. We went to tea with Heather's quilting friends. Sara made chocolate chip cookies for the occasion, and they were totally enjoyed by all. Afterwards, Heather took us to lunch and then to the market where we each found something interesting. I found a basket and a wooden coaster set. Sara found a skirt that she liked, and Heather talked to the lady that had made the chargers for me the previous Christmas.

Later in the afternoon, we went to high tea with Heather. It was a day of tea, and a wonderful surprise when Heather took us to a place called WILD IS LIFE. This is a rescue center for injured or orphaned animals, or animals that have been abused by people.

We were first introduced to two lions: a male and a female, both chewing on bones. The next resident that we met was an adorable little warthog named Pickles. She loved to walk close by the lion cage and tease the lions.

We were waiting for some other guests to arrive before going to the lions, who were waiting to be fed. One lions name was George, and apparently the owner had bottle fed him as a baby and had let him live in the house. Angela, our hostess, said that the owner came out to see George at least once a week. In the meanwhile, we were served tea and cookies and cakes.

We also met Holly, the baby baboon who was a pill. She was tied to a tree to limit her range. She was very quick and tried to grab anything that was not tied down or attached. She tried to grab my watch and camera strap and had a very strong grip. She was still being bottle fed.

The absolute best animal of all was Heather's special surprise for me. When they brought out the Pangolin, I was so excited, even ecstatic to see her. Most people don't get to see a Pangolin ever in their lifetime, and that includes guides. This little Pangolin had her own keeper, who stayed with her all of the time and even went out ant hunting with her. She was held like a baby with her head up over the caretaker's shoulder. All of a sudden, she whipped her tongue out about 6 inches and flicked it about. That must have meant that she was hungry because the caretaker put her down to go scavenge for ants. She took off on her 2 back legs and held her front legs up, somewhat like a Kangaroo. She then stopped to dig down in the dirt a bit and then stuck her long tongue down into an ant hole and started sucking up the ants, which then started coming out of the hole by the hundreds. They were running all over her. When she had finished, the caretaker picked her up and put her back in his backpack. She turned herself around so that just her nose was peeking out. It was the experience of a lifetime to observe her behaviors. I was beyond thrilled, since I love Pangolins. They are so unique and very endangered. The Chinese are the worst country to capture and kill them for their scales.

Sweet Pea was the resident Kudu. She was about 17 years old and the owners and caretakers had totally spoiled her with sweets. The patio area was separated with the outer part being a concrete pad and the inner part, under the patio covering, a more slippery treated concrete. Sweet Pea joined us with her hooves just up to the edge of the slippery part and with neck stretched out as far as possible, she reached for some morsel from someone's hand; all the while sticking her tongue partially out and making a sucking noise as if to suck whatever was in someone's hand into her mouth. She was very gentle and friendly, and of particular interest to all of us. I gave Sweet Pea two bites of cake, which she loved, and she begged for more. Pickles on the other hand, was happily searching for dropped morsels from under the table. Even the dogs joined her under the table at one point. The dogs were very annoying but apparently their role was to keep the baby baboon, Pickles, and Moyal, the baby elephant, happy.

After our tea, we were taken around the garden and told more about each animal. Then Angela had the caretaker bring out Moyal. He was tiny and so adorable. We all fell instantly in love with him. He was about 6 months old and weighed about what a normal newborn elephant would weigh. Angela said that he had been born prematurely, and was found after a flood had apparently washed him down stream. Moyal means Strong Heart. He had a little red blanket over him, and the caretaker took it off of him for a while and led him to his play box which was filled with a mountain of dirt with wood shavings at the base of the 3-foot-high mountain. It was so entertaining to watch him jump up and down and kick dirt up and all over himself with his feet and trunk. Next, he ran down his little mountain and turned round and round, making the shaving crackle. He was wild with excitement.

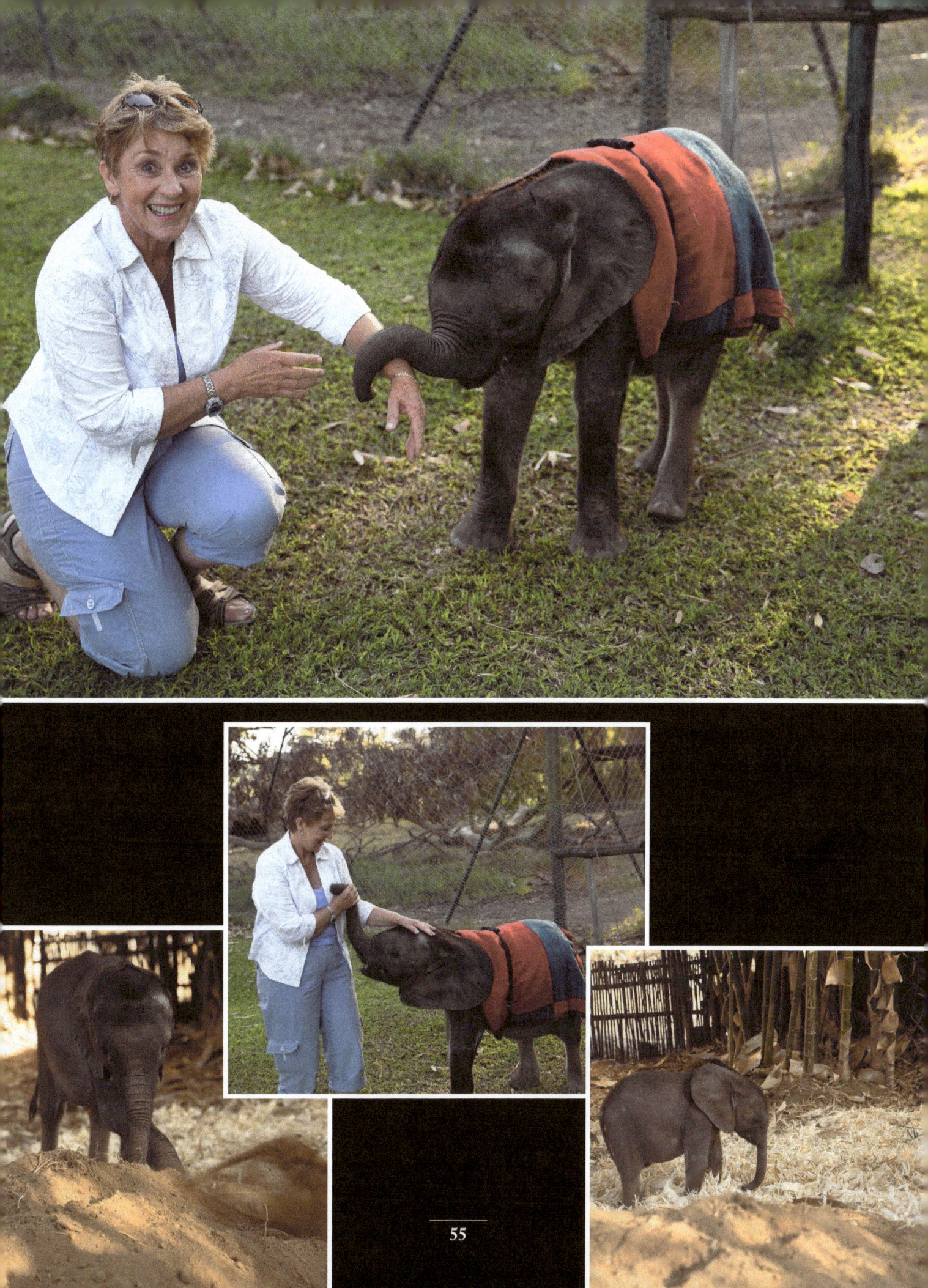

Our next visit was to the Cheetahs. There were 2 male brothers and one female. Because Cheetah are so endangered, these were the only animals at Wild is Life, that the owners had tried to get to mate. The female didn't like one of the brothers, and the other one tried to take a bite out of her. Therefore, no babies are planned for the future. Angela had told our group that we would each get a personal encounter with the Cheetah, as long as she allowed us to get close and personal. She allowed Heather, Sara, and I to all get to pet her… and then she was done. Everyone else was very disappointed.

Among the other animals that we saw, were the giraffe, who were huge, but were still juveniles. We each got a turn to bottle feed them. They were slobbery with their very long tongues, but it was a fun and different experience.

July 24, 2014—We were off to the airport to fly to Mana Pools in Stretch's camp. We arrived at 3PM and after settling in our tents, we went out on a game drive to see all of the animals. We saw the usual resident elephants, elands, Kudus, impalas, and a lion who had been quite beaten up by his Dad and uncles because he didn't want to leave the pride and be on his own. Mama's boy.

We also saw some waterbucks, baboons, and several varieties of wild birds. Not enough room in this book for everything. We also saw hippos and crocs. The hippos were very noisy through the night. Stretch teased Sara about her lip piercing and her different colored nails.

Stretch signalling a bull elephant to stop and not charge him and Sara. One of these days an elephant will decide to charge anyway if he doesn't like the look of one of the guests. In my opinion, this is a very dangerous practice. There are several elephants such as Fred Astaire, that stand up on their back legs to reach the tender new leaves at the top of the Acacia trees. In a drought, he will also allow some of the babies to eat, but never a younger bull or rarely the mother of the elephant calf. Very interesting behaviors to watch.

This is the last day of our trip to Mana Pools. We have had a wonderful time and enjoyed seeing so many new things and new places along the way… We enjoyed seeing Stretch again and being in his camp. Until next time…